Michael

More blessings for
you from this God's
2nd book of poems.

God's love & More
ED Bhagatt

Betty McDonnell

"More" From God's Heart, To Mine, To Yours

Book 2

E. P. Shagott

WESTBOW
PRESS
A DIVISION OF THOMAS NELSON
& ZONDERVAN

Scripture taken from the King James Version of the Bible.

Scripture taken from the New King James Version®. Copyright © 1982 by Thomas Nelson. Used by permission. All rights reserved.

WestBow Press books may be ordered through booksellers or by contacting:

WestBow Press
A Division of Thomas Nelson & Zondervan
1663 Liberty Drive
Bloomington, IN 47403
www.westbowpress.com
1 (866) 928-1240

ISBN: 978-1-9736-5174-1 (sc)
ISBN: 978-1-9736-5175-8 (e)

Print information available on the last page.

WestBow Press rev. date: 1/31/2019

Salvation

The title of this poem is salvation,
a word that says it all.
For within it's nine letters you will find
life's answers since the fall.

Love, hope, praise, and honor
contentment, peace is there.
These are also some of the words
that we seek when asking in prayer.

Each one of us must seek salvation out,
for surely sin is not the way.
And through Jesus Christ, the Son
our God cares for us today.

Humiliated, despised and riddled with shame,
yes, these words are in there too.
His Son was nailed to the cross
so salvation could be there, for me and you.

So please, don't take this word lightly
and pray that all might find,
that because of the price He paid for us,
not one has to stay behind.

It's Time To Come Home

How do I call an end
to a love that's embedded in my heart?
How do I say good-bye
to someone who's been there from the start?

How do I stop this pain
that never seems to go away?
Can someone tell me what to do
to make life easier today?

What is left to hold on to?
What direction is there for me to go?
My life was built around you,
because I loved you so.

I know if things were different
and I was the first to leave
I would be waiting at Heaven's gate,
as I know you are for me.

Our life on earth is temporary,
a gift from our Master above,
Just think of what He endured
to show us His true love.

Please wait for me, my loved one
for I know I'll never be alone
and I'll be waiting just to hear
Jesus say, "It's time to come home".

Live Each Day With Love

Its hard to comprehend
how time has passed.
Years, months, days gone by
with only the memories to last.

Missed opportunities and chances
to say what was needed to hear.
Missed moments in time
for actually being there.

So what was it all about?
Why did we do what we did?
It is all in the past now,
it is how we chose to live.

What the future holds for us,
only the Lord knows above.
The future is today and tomorrow,
to live each day with love.

I'll Remember

I'll remember your smile
and your caring ways
your loving touch
and the sunshine filled days.

I'll remember your eyes
as I looked to see
that devotion they showed
because of your love for me.

I'll remember your presence
every time you were near
all the kisses and hugs,
that you gave me, dear.

I'll remember each moment
that was blessed from above,
each one the Lord did give us
which we shared through our love.

Now that you're no longer with me
there is one thing so true
when the Lord calls me home
I'll once again be with you.

As I Walked Into Heaven

As I walked into Heaven, I looked around
for a friend I wanted to see.
From a distant I saw this figure
of someone coming closer to me.

There was warmth in the smile
and comfort on this face,
which made me feel so at ease
upon entering this place.

Though I never felt worried
or unsure at any time,
I was truly hoping
it would be a friend of mine.

So as this figure drew nearer
more light began to shine,
my new heart started beating faster
could I really be meeting Jesus, for the first time?

What would I do
or what will I say?
The moment I always dreamt of on earth,
was not that far away

(continued on next page)

I wanted to run up
but also wanted to fall to my knees!
Closer and closer the figure came
closer and closer to me.

How would I begin to say
all that has been in my heart?
How do I give thanks for all the love
that was always there right from the start?

Through all the Bible readings
and all the lessons learned,
it is now about to be made known
for which my soul has always yearned.

Praise to You, Lord Jesus
for the price You had paid
for if not for You
there would never be this day.

Peace, love, contentment
and never again to be alone!
I am now with my Savior,
I am now finally home!

Why

Days and nights come and go
sunshine disappears,
some flowers bloom and then they die
yet while others reappear.

Children ask us questions
and many answers we do not know.
Some roads are smooth, some bumpy,
oh where did the sunshine go?

Some people hurt more than others,
yet many may never cry.
Still in our ever changing life
should we stop to ask why?

There is a question, please don't ask,
for the answer you should already know.
My thoughts and prayers are always with you
and always remember, God loves you so!

On A Hill Far Away

On a hill far away
a young man went.
Because of His Fathers love,
His Son was sent.

From His first day on earth
so many years ago,
born a virgin birth
pure and white as winters snow.

He was beaten and bruised,
despised and shamed.
And as He hung on the cross,
He knew each of our names.

Forgive them Father,
they heard Him say,
as His last words were spoken
on a hill far away.

God Gave Me A Heart

God gave me a heart
to love just like Him
God gave me this heart
to keep family and friends in.

God gave me a heart
to feel good and feel sad
God gave me this heart
to forgive when I am mad

God gave me a heart
to use when in doubt
God gave me this heart
so I would have a way out.

God gave me a heart
so I would always know
God gave me this heart
because He loves me so.

God gave me a heart
so a place He could be
God gave me this heart
so He is always with me.

Some Days

Some days everything is thrown upon you,
Some days you can give it all back,
Some days you get to throw first,
Some days who cares, for there's nothing left!

Some days hurt more than others,
Some days there is no pain,
Some days we walk in sunshine,
Some days it's just pouring rain!

Some days I think of no one,
Some days I just think of family and friends,
Some days seem to go by so fast,
Some days never seem to end!

Some days are just very boring,
Some days just don't pay,
Some days I sit and write poetry,
Some days just like today!

T'was The Month
We Celebrate Christmas

T'was the month we celebrate Christmas
and not many would still understand,
that the reason for this season
is the beginning of God's plan.

He knew there would be so many,
to walk each day in doubt.
So He came to us in person
to show us His way out.

Yes, it started as a baby
as all of us do,
and 33 years later
proved His love for me and you.

So each day in December
as that special day draws near,
please take the time to understand
how blessed you were this year!

Blessed because He cares for you
and knew this life will end.
Blessed because He loves you so,
for on Christmas, His Son, He did send.

My Eyes Gazed At The Cross

As I walked into church
and sat in my favorite pew,
my eyes gazed at the cross
and I didn't know what to do.

I envisioned Jesus nailed to it
and heard Him say to me,
"I am glad you came to My house,
it is important for Me, you see!

Sometimes in your busy life
you never take time to understand.
See everything you hear, taste, touch and smell
was all created for you,
by these nail pierced loving hands!

Remember Sunday is My day
to come learn, sing and give Praise.
For yes, it is I, Jesus,
that is with you each and every day.

So thank you for coming to My house,
this visit is always short and sweet.
I can't wait to thank you in person,
on the day we finally meet!"

Sitting In The Same Pew

Two people went into church
and then sat in the same pew,
one heard the preacher's sermon
the other thought of things to do.

One person gave their tithe
as the elders passed the plate,
The other person looked away
and thought all they do here is take.

When the pastor said the church needed help,
one person thought what could I do?
The other just raised their eyes and thought
here they come again, they're always after you.

Two people walked into church that day,
but sitting side by side they were so far apart.
The difference was not in God's church,
but what was truly in their heart.

Did I Tell You, Thank You Lord

Did I tell You, "thank You Lord"
when I first awoke from sleep?
Did I tell You, "thank You Lord"
for in my heart your presence I keep.

For all the many blessings
because of Your Grace I do receive,
did I tell You, "thank You, Lord"
for in me You do believe?

Did I tell You, "thank You Lord"
for never giving up on me?
Even when friends and family
seemed content to just let me be.

For all those minutes, hours, and endless days
that could be empty as can be,
did I tell You, "thank You Lord"
for being that special one to me?

Well if for some reason I didn't,
please forgive me once again!
"Thank You Lord, for the beginning,
the in between, for with You there is no end!

Life's Seasons

Just as the leaves fall from the trees,
life can change for you and me,
one time happy, another time sad,
very quickly you have less than you had.

One day very healthy
and the next very, very sick,
just like the various seasons,
life can change very quick.

Friends by the numbers,
then suddenly very few,
part of life's seasons,
the old and the new.

So thanks to you, Jesus,
being the same from the start,
as life's seasons come and go,
only yours stays true in my heart.

Throne Of Grace

I was called to the Throne of Grace
for my life God wanted to review.
With His loving Son sitting by His side
God said, "What was done with the gifts I gave to you?"

It was for sure God knew the answers
to each question that He asked of me.
But He waited very patiently
for the answer I would give you see.

My body started to tremble
as I struggled with what to say.
I've heard this mentioned in many sermons
that the Pastor spoke of in so many ways.

Gifts like wisdom, knowledge, faith,
healings, prophecy and tongues,
my mind was searching franticly,
what did I have, was it many or just one?

As I raised my head to answer,
Jesus looked down from the throne above,
He looked over to our Heavenly Father
and said, "Father this child is special
because of his love!"

"Remember the many wounded, lost and hurting
that so many others just let be?
Each and everyone you touched with love, my child,
you were actually touching Me!"

Back To Calvary

An angel of the Lord
came and said to me,
"I want to take you back
to a place called Calvary."

So back through time we went,
the Lord's angel and me,
back before all time that passed
back to that special place, named Calvary!

Though I knew of this place
from the Bible I did read,
I was so excited to be there
where our Lord died for you and me.

As I stood very still
with the Lords angel at my side,
I really didn't notice anyone but Jesus
as He looked into my eyes.

In my heart I felt His suffering,
in my eyes I saw His pain,
and through it all He smiled at me
and then He said my name.

I fell to my knees and said,
"Lord so many just don't see
the love you have for all of us
and the importance this place is, called Calvary."

Closer To The Lord

I went up to the mountaintop,
so closer to the Lord I could be.
My eyes looked in all directions
but my Savior I did not see.

I thought maybe if I yelled
from the top of my lungs,
the Lord would hear my voice
and see how far I'd come.

So as I stood and waited
for my Savior to appear,
I let my heart be still
and waited without fear.

And then within the moment
in my heart He did speak.
Jesus said, "My child,
what is it that you seek?"

I felt His presence in my spirit,
and said, "My Lord with You I want to be!"
Jesus' love touched me deeply and replied,
"I am with you always, even in the valleys."

Jesus said, My Spirit is within you
no matter where you roam,
His love is the same as the Father's and Mine,
and through Our love it will bring you home.

Do You Feel His Presence

The amazing part of God's love is
no matter where you are,
He is always there with you
not distant from afar.

Do you feel His presence?
Are you unsure when you speak?
Do you still think He is just for
the lost and the weak?

Are you still like so many
that want Him in your heart,
but struggle with each passing day
wondering how do I start?

I believe God is just waiting
for you like He did with me.
Do you feel His presence?
Are you longing to be free?

Well, if you are like most
and waiting on God you must be,
please understand He is waiting for you,
just like He did with me.

Please don't wait too long
for the next minute could be your last,
and eternity you couldn't spend with Him,
all because you did not ask!

Sacrifice

As I passed by a grave site
I heard a voice whisper to me.
Please stop for just a moment
and realize why you are so free.

I was a young soldier
fighting and alone.
I sacrificed all I had
so you could have what we call home.

All I ask is you take time,
to be thankful as can be,
for it was also because of their sacrifice
others gave, just like me.

So now if you're wondering
if all our work is done?
No, for we are now in God's army of angels,
still protecting you all, one by one.

See God also paid the sacrifice
and He, like us, prays it was not for naught.
We the soldiers for your freedom
and Christ for your salvation on the Cross.

We Are To Be His Eyes, Ears, Hands And Feet

With my eyes I am looking for sinners,
yes, people just like me.
With my heart is where I keep Jesus
because He first loved me.

So everyday I find one,
a sinner lost and looking to be free,
I tell them of my friend Jesus
and what He did for me.

He took away my hurting,
He filled my heart with love,
He gives work for me to do for Him
until that day we're together above.

So with my ears I will listen,
with my eyes I will definitely seek,
with my hands I will embrace them
that He brings me to, with my feet.

They being the sinners,
yes, the ones just like me.
All they have to do is choose,
so with Him they can also be.

What More Can I Do

How can I reach them, Lord,
please tell me what more can I do?
It appears the harder I try
the farther they get away from You.

I try to show them by Your example,
from the Bible I quote Your Word.
It's like telling them of something
that most have never heard.

What can I do, Lord,
to help them understand
everything they are destroying on earth
was created by Your own loving hands?

Please understand, Lord,
I'm not giving up on You.
You are the most important person in my life,
I just want everyone to feel that way too!

He Is The Light

"There is light at the end of the tunnel",
is a saying I heard someone say.
But did you ever walk in darkness
with no light to show the way?

Each step is always uncertain
for you don't know what lies ahead.
Oh, for just a little light to shine,
to remove this fear and dread.

Then all of a sudden a voice
spoke clearly to my heart.
"Do not be afraid, child of Mine
for with Me there is no dark!

The light is always there,
for with your heart to see.
The darkness is from your mind,
the light is from your heart, that is truly Me!"

The Face In The Mirror

I looked in the mirror
and what did I see,
the face of Jesus
looking back at me.

I said, "Oh Lord,
how can this be?
The things I've done
You can't really want to be me!

You never sinned
or did any wrong,
How can I possibly think
being with You I belong?"

Then within a moment
He spoke to my heart.
"The past is forgiven
let Me be your new start!

If you can say yes
and finally agree,
then the reflection in the mirror
will always be Me."

What A Friend I Have In Jesus

To all my friends and family,
who think with me, Jesus is just a trend.
Please remember when I tell you
He is the beginning, not the end!

My walk will only strengthen
as each day comes and goes,
for my life is now His,
and this Jesus truly knows.

So please take time to read these emails,
that He is speaking through me to you.
For His mission for me is awesome,
and there is so much He wants me to do.

This year is almost over,
and is almost at its end.
If you thought I loved Him this year,
wait until next year, my friends!

Final Journey

The trip was a little bumpy,
as I was leaving earth.
I heard a lot of voices,
more then was at my birth.

One voice said, "I wish there was
more that we could do!"
Another one said sadly,
"So much for someone to go through."

The farther away we got,
the quieter it became.
Then very softly I heard
the Savior call my name.

Though there were others with me
who left at just the same time,
some were being taken to a different place,
Jesus said, "No not that one, he is mine!"

Each one was looking at Jesus,
for they now did understand,
some the trip would start getting bumpier,
the others were headed to the promise land.

The ones that were not chosen
cried out, "How can this be?"
Jesus said, "The decision was yours,
you chose something, but it was not me!"

The Baby Cried

The baby cried, and God spoke
amid the hay on the ground.
The King of Kings lay in a manger
with animals all around.

The baby cried, the Lord did speak
but not many did hear the sound.
Just Mary, Joseph and three wise men
with the animals gathered around.

The baby cried, it was the Great I Am,
and that sound you can hear today.
The Angels voices rang from Heaven,
Christ was born in Bethlehem, so far away.

The baby cried, and the Savior said,
"I Am the Holy One."
Then God the Father spoke to all,
"Behold my glorious Son!"

Dear friends and family please listen close
to hear this baby's cry!
The sound of love that He did speak,
was meant for you and I!

What Can It Be

What is it that makes me want
to write poems and sing to Thee?
What is that makes me long for You,
please tell me Lord, what can it be?

Why am I so consumed,
to search for You every morning, noon and night?
Please tell me Lord what more can I do,
to be more pleasing in Your sight?

What can it be that makes me want,
to reach out to You above?
With my eyes I am always looking,
with my ears, listening for Your Words of love.

I know the answer will come one day
when we stand together face to face,
then I will know and understand
when my Savior I finally embrace!

Then And Now

Many, many years ago,
back in the Garden of Eden,
Adam and Eve, because of their sin,
from God's eyes they wanted to be hidden.

Though God called out to each of them
and knew exactly where they were,
Adam and Eve's sin seemed so much greater
than the relationship with God they wanted to share.

Though many days have passed since then
and in this world sin is still all around,
God is still calling out to you and me
and knows exactly where we are to be found.

Please listen to His Words of love
and ask Him to forgive you of your sin,
make sure to give thanks to Jesus, His Son,
a relationship we can have today, just because of Him!

It Is All About Love

It is all about love,
no matter what you do.
It is love that starts your day
and is love that gets you through.

Love was at the very beginning,
when God spoke, "Let there be light."
Yes love was there each time we failed,
but we remained so precious in His sight.

Even as the worldly sin increased,
His love would not let go.
Each time His flesh was cut so deep,
He said, "Father forgive them", because He loved us so.

And His love was left within us,
on that day from this world He did depart.
The same love that was in the beginning,
remains embedded so deep inside our hearts.

God Created A Mom

God gave her loving hands,
to grab and hold us tight.
God gave her a gentle heart,
to guide and make things right.

God gave her understanding,
for He knew with children she would need.
God gave her endurance and patience,
all needed to raise a family!

God gave her eyes to watch,
and ears to hear our cries.
God gave her many answers,
to all our many questions and whys???

But what was most important,
was His love for each and everyone,
see God created "a mom",
to see the job got done!

It Was Not Me

I opened my mouth to speak,
but it was not me.
I looked out of these worldly eyes,
but I really could not see.

I reached out with sinful hands
to grab from all I could.
With my ears I listened to Satan's lies,
no wonder my life was not good.

So I got down on my knees,
and said, "Jesus, what can I do?"
Jesus spoke to my heart and said,
"Let me be all of you!"

So now Christ and I are one
and I finally understand,
ever since God said, "Let there be light",
I was always in His plan!

Broken And Victorious

When I realized I was broken,
I made my greatest gain.
The victory didn't come in triumph,
but rather through my pain.

How can that be you might ask,
to win when you have lost?
Oh my beloved and precious one,
Jesus taught me that through the cross.

Each one of us must learn to be humble,
to understand we can't do it on our own.
Cry out to our Creator, "Help me!",
as He sits upon His Throne.

The Father's eyes are upon us,
His ears are listening for our pleas.
Just as He heard His Son cry out from the cross,
Praise His Holy Name, I know He can hear me.

My Decision

I woke up this morning
and had a decision to make.
Do I go through this day
for mine or for Christ's sake?

Do I grab all I can,
or give from the heart?
A choice I must make
before my day would start.

I must decide
before my day begins,
what will I choose,
will it be for me or for Him?

Lord, please guide my decision
as I decide what to do.
May it be the best choice I can make,
and may it be all about You!

Before And After

This life is always changing,
each day brings something new.
What once was bright and shining,
with time turns dull, it's true.

Just like our earthly bodies,
that once were tight and firm,
we can now look in a mirror,
and see from time what we have learned.

Is there anything that will stay the same,
as through life we do proceed?
Yes my friends, it's called God's love,
given by His grace to you and me.

See it was there from the beginning,
and will be there in the end.
A gift for each and everyone,
all you have to do is choose, my friend.

Life's Rivers

I came to one of life's rivers,
looking for a place to cross.
I had to get to the other side
for I felt where I was, all was lost.

I looked over to the other side
and saw Jesus waving to me.
I cried out, "Here I am Lord,
please come and help me!"

I heard Him speak in a very loud voice,
"Do not be afraid and don't lose heart.
There is a time and place for you to cross,
and we will never be apart.

Life's rivers are many,
trials that will come your way.
Just have faith and trust in Me,
and we will cross them together each day!"

God Is Waiting For You To Choose

Do not think that God is waiting,
to see what you are going to do.
He already knows your heart,
and everything there is about you.

He is not waiting for you
to do some kindly deed,
for He knows what is in your heart,
and exactly what you want to do indeed.

God is not waiting on you,
to once in a while sing His praise,
for God already has all the answers,
as we live throughout our days.

What God is waiting for
is for you to make that choice,
to surrender your life totally to Him
and you listen carefully to His Spirit's voice.

So as each day quickly goes by,
you may have lost another time
to choose to start a new life in Christ,
for I chose, and He is the best friend of mine!

The Test

My heart is at unrest,
day after day,
as I go through this life,
trying to find a better way.

What can be found,
to give me the peace,
to satisfy my heart,
that beats within me?

Each day is a struggle,
as we travel life's way.
Just another daily test,
then from His Word, I read today,

In Luke chapter 1, verse 79, to give light to those
who sit in darkness and in the shadow of death,
to guide our feet into the way of peace.
Jesus gave me the answer to life's test.

See, it doesn't matter
what life throws your way.
What is most important of all
is that Christ is the center of our day!

Luke 1 verse 79 - NKJV

Behold His Hands

Behold His hands so strong and true
that guide us through our day.
Hands that lift us when we fall,
and wipe our tears away.

Behold His hands of brotherhood
that reach out to everyone.
To seek and touch each lonely soul,
ever since their lives have begun.

Behold His hands of power,
that through Him keep us strong.
And by His hands that give us strength
to keep us from all wrong.

Behold His hands of tenderness,
that soothe each breaking heart.
These are the hands of God, my friends,
that have been with us from the start.

Behold His hands of suffering,
that were nailed to the tree.
These are the hands of Jesus,
The Lamb of Calvary!

Behold the hands of reassurance,
that never will let us go.
Behold the hands of the Trinity,
reaching out because They love us so!

In The Shadows Of Life

I stood in the shadows of life,
unnoticed to those passing by.
Just a plain, quiet person,
content to live and not question why.

I did what people asked me to,
never thinking of fortune or fame.
Content being in the shadows
is what my life became.

Then one day I heard of Christ
from a person just like me.
They were always quiet too,
but Jesus just wouldn't let them be.

See, once you learn of Jesus
and accept Him into your heart,
He brings you out from the shadows,
into His light, where you're never to be apart!

When You Look At Me

When you look at my face,
what do you see?
Because I love Jesus,
it is Him, really not me.

When I reach out to touch someone,
it is His hands that does.
They are reaching out to His lost
to be claimed for the Father above.

When my feet are carrying me
to places to give Him praise,
these are really the feet of Christ,
that carried me all my days.

When my mouth opens with song,
praising His Holy Name,
it is His Holy Spirit flowing from me,
touching lives that will never be the same.

So when you look at me,
take a good look at what you see,
my old being is gone,
it's now Jesus, not me!

I Want To

I don't have to but I want to
give Him praise every day.
I don't have to but I want to
let Him be my guiding light today.

I don't have to but I want to
listen to His Spirit as He speaks.
I don't have to but I want to
tell others about Him that I meet.

I don't have to but I want to
please Him in all I do.
I don't have to but I want to
reach out to others that need Him too.

I want to, not that I have to
love Him with all my heart.
I want to, not that I have to,
because He loved me first from the start!

Surrender To Him

Oh give to the Lord what He seeks,
surrender to Him what is His.
He cannot work through our lives,
until we willingly and truly do this.

We must admit to ourselves,
that we are weak and He is **the Way.**
We must surrender to Him all we are,
so that He can truly live in us today.

We can't hold back a single thing,
we must see **the Truth** in His Word.
We must surrender to Him our total being,
so through us His Gospel can be shared.

See, He was the first to surrender all for us,
so that **the Life** with Him will always be.
Surrender to Him our earthly lives,
as on the Cross He did for you and me.

The Choice Is Up To You

The choice is up to you,
just how you spend your time.
You can choose to live in sin,
fooling yourself everything is just fine.

You can choose to ignore
those less fortunate than you.
You can choose to believe
it's all about you, but that's not true.

The choice is definitely yours,
because God made it so.
But you better choose wisely,
before it's time to go.

God will always be waiting
and watching just what you do.
He has already made His choice,
now the choice is up to you.

My Life Is Being Tried

My life is always being tried
by my Savior, who is my God!
As each day passes I find some trials,
wherever my feet may begin to trod.

These trials may come as health problems,
or sometimes breakage of my heart.
But I know as a Child of His,
where I go we are never apart.

What these trials are doing
is testing my resolve in Him.
They're bringing my soul closer to Godliness,
without them where do I begin?

These trials are meant to exercise my faith
in my Lord that my eyes cannot see.
My life is always being tried,
all because of His love for me.

Poetry

Poetry is the heart singing,
it comes from deep within.
When you hear these words of love,
they really come from Him.

It is a way to tell all, He loves them.
A way to touch each and every heart.
It is a flowing of His Spirit,
like when David would play his harp.

So please don't close your ears
to His love songs that the poetry brings.
It is a way to speak to each one of us,
and His special message that He wants to bring.

To the ones that He has chosen,
to write down His Words of love,
it is because we want to do so,
as we give praise to the Father above.

Pray Without Ceasing

Pray without ceasing,
means just what it says.
Just because your prayer isn't answered,
doesn't mean it won't be answered later ahead.

God is not just working
for and with you,
there are so many other things
that He has to first get done, it is true.

We are only looking for
what we need at that time.
God is seeing the whole picture
and it is sure the answer He will find.

So keep praying without ceasing,
always thanking Him for what He is to do.
Remember the answer to your prayer,
is to bring glory to Him, not you!

With His Last Breath

With His last breath taken,
Jesus looked down from the cross.
He was looking throughout all time,
always reaching out for all the lost.

His eyes were constantly searching,
looking into each earthly heart.
As His last breath was quickly leaving,
knowing very quickly He would have to part.

Jesus wants for all men and women,
who truly believe in Him,
to pick up their own cross of salvation,
and tell others, so they can be born again.

So with His last breath taken,
He said, "Father, it is finished, Your will is done."
Now my friends it is up to you and me,
to reach out to His lost before our last breath comes.

Temptation

Very often throughout our days,
we are being tempted to do something bad.
It is most important when you are,
to just resist with all you have.

Don't let even a single bad thought
enter in your mind and then take hold.
Resist, resist with all your might,
for in the Bible that is what we are told.

Always keep Jesus as our example,
as tempted by Satan in the Bible we did read.
Though being human at that time many years ago,
Jesus told him, "It is written, flee from Me!

So as we go through our daily lives,
let's stay focused on what is true.
Listen to what the Holy Spirit is saying,
and temptation won't be able to affect you.

Is About

Christianity is about love.
Christianity is about the truth.
Whether you believe that or not
is really all up to you.

The Father is about mercy.
The Father is about grace.
His wonderful love now flows out to us,
because of our sins, Jesus took our place.

Jesus is about salvation,
Jesus is about healing too.
When He went to the cross,
it was because of me and you.

The Holy Spirit is about teaching.
The Holy Spirit is about guiding us too.
So pick up and read the Bible, my friends,
for there you will find, it is all so very true.

Wait, Just Wait

When a problem arises,
what are you to do?
Wait, just wait,
is what the Lord is telling you.

The pain is so strong,
the hurt just doesn't leave.
Still wait, just wait,
The Lord says, "Wait on Me."

But how can we wait,
Why is it necessary, what can it be?
God wants us to always need Him,
is what I truly believe.

The longer the wait,
the greater is the need.
Keep your focus on Him,
Wait, just wait, and you will finally see.

The Debt Was Paid

He carried that cross
for you and for me,
knowing that soon
He would be nailed to that tree.

He felt that spear
as it pierced His side,
and when nothing was left,
water flowed from inside.

He saw all the people,
that looked at Him in disgrace,
as the blood from the thorns
streamed down on His face.

But what hurt Him the most,
even more than the beatings, you see,
was looking to His Father and saying,
"My God, My God, why have You forsaken me?"

So when it's your time to leave,
please do not be afraid,
sin will no longer separate us from God,
because of Jesus, the debt was paid!

His Message, Is In The Poem

I started to write the words,
from my heart that which did flow.
Some lines ended in rhyme,
which made it into a very nice poem.

It's substance was of love,
and how God cares for you and me.
His Words flowed from Heaven above,
all about setting the captives free.

For He knows what is our bondage,
and what fills our lives with sin.
He wants for us to release that,
so in our hearts He can enter in.

So take some time to read this,
and think of how much you owe Him.
I hope you can understand
His message, is in the poem.

Jesus Is Waiting On You

What a friend I have in Jesus,
He is always there for me.
If I fall He lifts me up,
when so many would just let me be.

What a friend I have in Jesus,
He forgives me when I am wrong.
It is no wonder I sing His praises,
for He fills my heart with song.

What a friend I have in Jesus,
He will never leave my side.
In His rest is where you'll find me,
for it is there I lose my foolish pride.

What a friend I have in Jesus,
He wants to be your friend too.
All you have to do is ask Him,
my friend Jesus, is waiting on you.

Tomorrow

I did not want tomorrow to come,
for I knew the pain would be so great.
But then I thought of Jesus' last night,
and the pain He endured for my sake.

I did not want tomorrow to come,
for it would be filled with anxiety and fear.
But then I thought of how my Savior must have felt,
knowing it had to come, so He could draw me near.

I did not want tomorrow to come,
I just wanted to run someplace and hide.
But then I felt the presence of the Father,
almost like He was right here at my side.

His Spirit spoke within my heart and said,
"Tomorrow must come, that's the way it must be.
You will never face another tomorrow alone,
we will face it together,
you, the Holy Spirit, Jesus and Me!"

Mending A Broken Heart

God looked down from Heaven
and saw a child of His hurting so.
He called for the angel in charge of hearts
and said, "You got some mending to do down below."

The angel walked up to the window
and said, "Father which one will it be?"
The Father pointed and said, "That child of Mine,
He has been crying out to me!"

So the angel nodded in obedience
and then started on his way.
Within seconds there was a knock on my door,
the angel said, "I am here to help you today!

I know your heart has been broken,
I was sent from the Father above.
I have just what you will need to mend,
it was a heart bag filled with love.

So he reached in and brought out family,
then a lot of friends he brought out too.
Next I saw the Pastor from church,
the angel smiled and said, "See, they all love you."

Then he said, "This last one is very special,
it comes from your Father above.
It is what completes the mending process,
for nothing mends a broken heart, like Jesus' love.

I Live By Faith

I live by faith
and God's true Word.
I speak His gospel,
so it could be heard.

I live by faith,
through His great love,
to share with many,
His blessings from above.

I live by faith,
yes, sight unseen.
I am Spirit led,
for on Christ I lean.

I live by faith,
not through worldly eyes.
For it is by faith,
He hears my cries.

One day will come,
I know it's true,
because of my faith,
Lord, I'll be complete in You!

We Are As One

We are as One,
the Lord and me,
through the Cross,
loved and free.

We are as One,
each breath We take
is for the Kingdom,
another lost soul to save.

We are as One,
that's the way it should be.
Living as One,
Jesus and me.

We are as One,
you can also be,
just say in your heart,
Jesus, be One with me!

A Prayer

I sent a prayer
to God above,
and asked it be blessed
by His grace and love.

I then did wait
to hear from Him,
for I knew I must be still
and be quiet within.

Whatever the result,
that He will send,
I know will bring glory
and honor to Him.

For answered prayer
is what He does.
Trust and obey
is all up to us.

I Have A Heart For God

I have a heart for God
that I display for all to see.
I am not ashamed to say,
"My Lord died for you and me."

I have a heart for God,
that reaches out to the lost.
I am not ashamed
to kneel before the Cross.

I have a heart for God,
because He first had a heart for me.
I am not ashamed
to say this publicly.

I have a heart for God,
someday it will beat as One.
I am not ashamed
to praise the Father, the Spirit and the Son!

Are You Ready To Receive

There was a man who couldn't walk,
who waited by the temples door.
Every day he would wait and wait,
hoping for alms, someone would give him more.

Then came Peter and John to him,
Jesus' love flowed from their eyes.
"Silver and gold I have none," said Peter,
"but what I have I give you, in Jesus name, arise."

So this lame man whom never walked since birth,
walked through the temple's doors.
He started worshiping and praising God,
which he never did before.

See the moral of the poem,
and the truth from the Bible believe,
"There is power in the name of Jesus,
if, my friends, you are ready to receive!"

The Fire Within

My heart was cold
from this world of sin.
Jesus said, "What you need,
is a fire within!

It starts with a spark,
then will grow with love,
the fuel you need
will come from above."

With my chilled heart
I cried, "Lord, let it be,
please through Your love,
ignite a spark in me!"

Then within a second,
the chill began to fade.
The spark was lit,
through Jesus' name!

So in this life,
it's not too late to begin,
all you need
is the fire within!

The Blessing

It is only a blessing
that when we receive,
we give thanks above
because we believe.

The blessing only comes,
because of His grace,
not of what we've done,
or said in it's place.

His blessings will flow,
to bring glory to Him,
not because we're so
deserving, my friends.

Blessings are gifts
from the Father above,
only given out,
because of His love.

So if there's a blessing
that might come our way,
let's all remember to give thanks,
that God thought of us today!

A Heavy Heart

I started to rise,
a heavy weight I did feel.
As I started my day,
my joy, the devil wanted to steal.

I worried and fret,
didn't sleep much last night.
I just kept thinking,
tomorrow wouldn't be right.

My heart grew heavier,
as bad thoughts came in.
My joy was leaving,
making room for more sin.

I cried to the Lord,
"How can this be?"
He said in an instant,
"Just focus on Me!

Your heart was made,
for Me from the start,
all sin you let in,
makes for a very heavy heart."

Choose

As God looked down from Heaven,
an angel asked, "Which one did You choose?"
"All of them", God replied,
"for none of them have to lose.

I love them all so very much,
and have right from the very start.
My Son, Jesus, gave His life for them,
then sent His Spirit to each and every heart."

Then the angel looked confused,
as he looked down below.
The angel said, "Why do so many still sin?
Is it because they do not know?"

Then the God of all Creation,
smiled and gave a sigh,
"For those who heard the gospel message,
I can not answer why.

My Word was left to guide them,
and answer what they do not know.
Each one must either choose eternity with Me,
or with the devil below!"

I Am So Blessed

I took a break from all I do,
to stop awhile and think of You.
I lifted my eyes and looked above,
with my mouth I confessed, "Lord, it's You I love."

The pause in my day was oh so great,
it made me thankful and stop to appreciate,
"No matter what I am doing or where I go,
it's You and me, Lord, this I truly know.

Though time on the clock just passes by,
it doesn't matter how hard I try,
for if I'm working or resting too,
what matters most is my thoughts of You.

So thank You, Lord, for all You do,
for I don't know how I could ever get through.
Day after day, year after year,
I am so blessed that You stay so near!"

I Waited

I waited for my answered prayers,
but with my eyes I did not see.
I had faith that they would be heard,
because of God's love for me.

I waited for a little sign
that everything would be alright.
I had faith I would see a sign,
for I knew I was precious in His sight.

I waited throughout the day
and also the evening too.
I read from my Bible, prayers are answered,
if by faith you believe it's true.

So I lifted my eyes to Heaven,
and thanked my Father above.
For the waiting keeps me close to Him,
thus always increasing our bond of love.

Another One For Christ

I once was walking in darkness,
though the sun filled the day.
My heart was hard and calloused,
as I was traveling on my way.

I heard the Gospel message preached,
as I sat in church one day,
the preacher said, "God loves you, my friends,
you must believe He is the only way.

With your mouth ask for forgiveness,
for your sins you must repent.
Ask Jesus to forgive them and be your Lord and Savior,
then the Holy Spirit in your heart will enter in."

So I did as the preacher said to do,
the "sinners prayer" I did recite.
All the wrongs that were in my life,
through Christ were now made right.

My heart is no longer calloused,
it was softened with His love.
Another sinner came to Christ that day,
as Heaven's choir sang "Halleluiah" above!

Praise To God

I praise God in the morning,
when my eyes first open to light.
I praise Him in the evening,
when darkness turns into night.

I praise Him in the daytime,
as I go about my day,
for praising Him is what I do,
for I now, know of no other way.

I praise Him in my sufferings,
as pain in me begins.
I praise my Lord and Savior,
for there is no life without Him.

Praise to You, Heavenly Father,
and praise to the Holy Spirit too.
Praise to my Lord and Savior, Jesus,
because of His love, brought me to all of You!

A Family Of One

To all my brothers
and sisters in Christ,
stay true to His mission
and stay strong in the fight.

Keep reading His Word
both day and night,
for by doing this
it will make life right.

Do not give in
to all the worldly lies,
keep focus on Jesus
and Heaven as your prize.

Show His love to all others
that ask us all why?
Be ready, willing and able
without uttering a sigh.

Share the gospel with all
and whomever you meet,
be sincere in your words
to the many that you greet.

Don't compromise the Word
to the lost that you seek,
be compassionate to the weary,
confused and the weak.

Always walk in the Son–light,
stay away from the dark,
don't be discouraged by others,
remember Noah and the Ark.

Stay strong and stay faithful
as Christ from the start,
and always listen to the Spirit
that resides in your heart.

Remember you are not alone
and the battle will be won,
it was written in God's Word
since this life had begun.

So stay devoted and committed,
giving praise to the Son,
the victory is ours
because we're a family of One!

It Was Me

Today I saw a homeless person
looking for something to eat.
His shoes were torn and ragged,
exposing parts of his feet.

Then I saw an addict,
trying to once again get high.
His body was shaking so badly,
how would he ever get by?

Next I saw a family man,
out looking for a job.
His family needed food to eat,
their situation was looking bad.

A young girl was working as a prostitute,
her childhood just passed her by.
The innocent smile that once was there,
removed by this world of sin, why?

The Lord then spoke to my heart
and asked, "From all of these what did you see?"
With tears running down my face I replied,
"Lord, what I did see was once me!"

God's Task

God spoke to my heart,
He said, "I have a task for you.
All you have to be is obedient,
and trust I will get you through.

I have everything you will need
to accomplish what needs to be done.
Just listen to My Spirit
and always give praise to My Son.

Never get discouraged
or even stop to question why.
You were picked special for the task,
so don't quit before giving it a try.

I know you can do it,
for you are my special one.
Someday you will understand why,
when we meet and I say, "Well done!"

The Answer

I heard a knock on my heart,
Jesus said, "Are you there?
I wanted to let you know
the Father and I just heard your prayer.

We know what you are going through,
just wanted to let you know it will be all right.
Keep focusing on Us, as you go about your day,
and even throughout your night.

The answer you are looking for,
We will be sending by a friend.
Remember it may not be what you want to hear,
but is what you will really need to mend.

So you will hear many answers,
but look for the one that is so very true.
See the answer will come from the friend's heart,
for like Me, he loves you too!"

Share If You Care

Share if you care,
for this is what we must do,
we need each other
to help each one get through.

Don't go on your own,
for there are many that care,
life is about looking,
for all the others to share.

God made us each for a reason,
that only He knows for true,
besides being special to Him,
we are special to each other too.

So lets give thanks to our Creator,
remember to reach out if you dare,
so many are waiting for you,
to share if you care!

Be Silent And Still

I trust in the Lord,
I obey His will,
but what I find hard,
is to be silent and still.

When a heart is broken,
or an answer we need,
to be silent and still
is very hard indeed.

When a body is aching
and relief we need,
God says, "Be silent and still,
then you will receive."

See, the Lord knows all
that is just right for you.
So if He says, "Be silent and still",
then that's what we must do.

Give To Him

Give to Him what is truly His,
your life, your love, your soul.
Give to Him for He gave of Himself,
for all of us, so many years ago.

Give to Him, what He should have,
yes, your life and love do give.
A life that was created with purpose,
to belong to only just Him.

Give freely of yourself,
for you are a Child of His.
Give to Him your total devotion
and praise as long as you shall live.

Your life was created for Him,
to love, worship and adore.
See, once you make the choice to give,
it's His life, not yours anymore!

The Father Of The Faithful

The Father of the faithful
had to slay His own Son,
to prove to all believers
His love from day one.

His will for the Son
is the same for you and me,
obey the Father's will,
for that's the way it must be.

Yes, for He is the Father of the Faithful,
He is the Father of Love,
He is the Father of Creation,
the Father of Heaven above.

From Jesus' own lips,
the Father's beloved Son,
in prayer to the Father said,
"Not My will, but Thy will be done!"

The Son-light

I walked out into darkness,
a cloudy day was in sight.
Every place I looked,
nothing seemed to be right.

No smiles on the faces,
as people passed me by,
adults were constantly arguing,
the kids just stood and cried.

Too many people in a hurry,
as time clicked off the clock.
Life was passing them by,
for they never took time to stop.

This day was so depressing,
I said, "Lord how can this be?"
He touched my heart and answered,
"What they are all missing is the Son-light, Me!"

He Has What We Need

We don't like the hurting,
we don't like the pain,
there will always be sunshine,
there will always be rain.

We cry out when in trouble,
to the Father above,
but do we take the time
to thank Him for all His love.

We stumble in darkness,
we fail to see the light,
we often forget to say
all our prayers every night.

So what does this all mean?
What can't we see?
My friends, we are people,
that will always be in need.

So always give thanks,
because He has just what we need.
We don't have to do it on our own,
if only we just will believe!

Freely He Gives

He gives us so many gifts,
daily as we do live.
The only thing He asks of us
is freely our love to Him we give.

Yes, freely the blessings flow down on us,
even when we do not ask.
Like energy to get through our day,
and to complete our daily tasks.

He gives the gift of family,
and friends to cherish near.
The gift of peace within our hearts
to live each day without fear.

But the greatest gift of all,
when given, broke His heart in two,
He gave His only Son for us,
yes, that's how much He loves me and you!

True Rest

Stop for just a moment
and thank the Lord above,
for He is interested in you,
and blesses you with His love.

He never turns His back on you,
even when you think He did.
He loves you because you are you,
believe me, you are His.

There is no place you can go,
where He is not there too,
He is waiting minute by minute,
for you to choose Him too!

So if things are going wrong,
and your life seems all a mess,
call Him into your heart, my friend,
for that's where you'll find true rest!

God's Love

I was walking along one of life's smooth paths,
then all of a sudden I did fall.
God grabbed my hand and lifted me up
and said, "I heard you when you called."

I said, "I didn't call, it wasn't me,
I really don't know who You did hear."
God said, "Everyone falls now and then,
their hearts always cry out in fear.

Sometimes the heart cries are louder,
than any verbal sound at all.
See, the path doesn't have to be bumpy,
for you to stumble or fall.

Believe in Me with all your heart,
is what you have to do,
that way any time you fall,
My love will grab onto you!"

The Master And The Servant

The Master called in His servant
and said, "What will you do for me?"
The servant said in reply,
"Whatever You ask, whatever it can be."

The Master smiled with His approval,
and reached out His hand in love.
The servant fell to his knees,
and obediently looked at His Master above.

The Master said, "What I have is yours,
please come share all this with Me."
The servant said, "I don't understand,
Master, please explain, what could it be?"

The Master said, "I love you,
and have ever since the start!"
The servant said, "I don't have anything for You,
Master, all I have to give is just my heart."

The Master smiled again, then said,
"That is the greatest gift one can give.
I gave Mine for you a long time ago,
see, it is the only way for us truly to live!"

A Healthy Christian

I am a healthy Christian,
my body is God's home.
I cannot have it fall apart,
and leave Him all alone.

Our world is full of poison,
that is killing young and old.
It is important we watch what we eat,
so our bodies don't corrode.

We were given eyes to read labels,
so we can understand what is best.
Stay away from junk food,
and God will do the rest.

See, God gave us an immune system,
to fight what comes our way.
Please decide like I did,
and become a healthy Christian today!

Be Nice To Someone

Be nice to someone,
as you go about your way.
Remember you don't know
what is going on in their life today.

You may be happy,
starting the day off with a smile.
They may be having a pain
that's lasting for a long, long while.

You may be fortunate,
to be lacking for nothing.
They may be praying
that they receive just something.

You may feel healthy,
not a pain is made real.
They may be waiting
to see what a medical test reveals.

You may be blessed,
with family and friends at you side.
They may be looking for a place
to just run away and hide.

Yes, be nice to someone today,
for you don't know, if your life may change.
See, when you give someone else a smile,
it tells them you understand in exchange.

The Cries To Heaven

There came a loud explosion
to Heaven that the angels did hear.
They ran to the Father,
who told them not to fear.

He said, "These are cries to Me,
from the many voices down below.
They are in need of something,
even those, of Me, they still don't know.

They cry because they are hungry,
even though My Word was left to feed.
They cry because they are lonely,
for My love they refuse to receive.

They cry because they are lost,
wandering aimlessly about their day.
They still don't understand
that My Son, Jesus, is the Way.

So I will still answer their cries,
and listen carefully to their pleas,
but the cries that I am waiting for,
is when they express their love for Me!"

I Thank Him

I thank Him in the morning,
I thank Him still at night.
I thank Him for the bad things,
so through Him, I can make them right.

I thank Him for the air I breathe,
and for the light so I can see.
I thank Him for the food I eat,
and His love that comforts me.

I thank Him for a place to live,
and the clothes that are on my back.
I thank Him for His friendship,
and knowing through Him, I will never lack.

I thank Him for family and friends,
and also for His Word that I can read.
I thank Him because I love Him,
and I know He really loves me!

My Heart's Now In Heaven

My heart is now in Heaven,
for I gave it to the Lord.
He asked me for it many times,
through His love and His Word.

At first I was reluctant,
for I thought it belonged to only me,
but God said, "I created it,
that's the only way it can be free!"

So now I can truly understand,
all the loneliness that I had,
the emptiness is now filled
with His love that makes me glad.

He is in control now,
with Him I shall never lack.
My heart is now in Heaven,
all I had to do was give it back!

God's Turning Up The Heat

God is turning up the heat
that is building up in me,
He is building a bonfire in my heart
that is reaching out for all to see.

It starts as a kindling,
then His love just grows and grows.
I cannot contain it within myself,
for it is about Him for all to know.

The warmth from His heat is genuine,
His love is so sincere,
His fire speaks to all that will listen,
"I am your God, I Am here!"

So don't worry if you just feel a spark,
just make sure it does not leave.
My fire for Him is raging on,
for God's turning up the heat in me!

The Mirror Of My Soul

Did you ever wonder what your soul looks like?
Does it have a face just like you and me?
Since it is the most important part of us,
why is that with our eyes it cannot be seen?

Our exterior is just temporary,
in time it will definitely fade away.
But the soul, oh, the precious soul
is with us forever, that will never decay.

I do believe we can see it,
whenever we are willing to try.
Just take a look in the mirror,
and don't let your eyes fool you or lie.

The mirror of my soul is visible,
for all the others to see.
With mine I pray you see Jesus,
for that's what I truly want it to be.

So when you look at the mirror of your soul,
if you do not like what you see,
ask Jesus to change it for you,
for my friends, that's what He did for me!

God Knows Best

God knows best, not you nor I,
to get us through the day.
His ways are right, for sure not ours,
so with Him we must always stay.

He knows our every wanting,
before we even think we do.
He knows us better than ourselves,
for He is God, and that is true.

God knows best, each of life's tests,
that through them stronger we will be.
Yes, God knows best, more than all the rest,
because of His love for you and me.

We should listen to what He tells us,
and obey what He tells us to do.
For God knows best for each of us,
not just for now, but for each day through.

I Am A Man/Woman Of God

I am a man/woman of God,
I follow what He says,
I don't worry about tomorrow,
for He knows what lies ahead.

My life is all His now,
all I must do is obey.
I don't have to worry,
for God has my back each day.

I am a man/woman of God,
created by His own hands.
He has a purpose for my life,
as He has for every woman and man.

So if you want to be one too,
it doesn't take a great task;
All you have to do is ask Him,
See, He is waiting for you to ask!

Why Not I

Today I saw a homeless person,
life was passing him by.
I raised my head above and asked,
"Lord, why not I?"

Then I saw a single mom,
discouraged and cast aside.
Again I raised my head above and asked,
"Lord, why not I?"

Next a saw an addict,
losing everything for his need.
I looked away and thought,
thank God that isn't me.

But then I heard God's voice,
as He did speak to me,
"Life is but a choice,
what you chose, so it will be.

So far you have chose wisely,
My grace has fell on you.
See, it is there for everyone,
what it depends on, is what they choose."

Waiting For Us All

There was a knock on my heart,
I said, "Lord is it you?"
He said, "Yes my child,
I will be coming for you."

I said, "When, Lord, when?
When will it be?"
The Lord said, "I will let you know,
after My Father tells Me.

Be not in this world,
for many from it still don't see,
everything created by My Father,
belongs just to Me.

So keep watch My child,
and stay strong in My Word.
Be obedient to Me,
and with a strong voice be heard.

Tell them, tell them,
with the gifts you were given,
I'm coming back my child,
waiting for all believers, is wonderful Heaven!"

Reach Out For Me

Look out through your eyes,
for those hurting or in need,
reach out, reach out,
and touch their lives for Me.

Though you may be blessed,
and have more than you need,
reach out, reach out,
and give to them for Me.

You may be happy,
and content as can be,
but look for the sad in despair,
reach out and love them for Me.

Because you are blessed,
and know what it is to be free,
think of those in bondage,
reach out and lead them to Me.

Don't think of yourself,
but of others you see,
oh, please children of Mine,
reach out, reach out for Me!

God Has The Last Word

God has the last word,
not you and definitely not me.
He decides and directs our lives,
whatever He chooses it to be.

Oh, we have choices to make
and consequences there will be.
But always remember He has the final say,
Yep, that's the way it will always be.

He said, "Let there be light,"
and there was, so all could see.
He said, "I will make man in my own image,"
Guess what? That's you and that's me!

Jesus had the last Word,
"It is finished," is what He said.
Our victory lies in Him,
the Father and Heaven waits ahead!

Finally Home

I wandered through this earthly world,
for my home I wanted to find.
I stayed in a few loving spots,
but was not what I had in mind.

There could only be one special place,
where I no longer would be getting old.
One special Master that waited for me,
for He knew one day I would be finally home.

This Master of mine has a loving heart,
so He decided with others to share.
Every day that I was so far away,
He patiently waited for me there.

See what is truly so amazing,
is His love for all the others too.
How awesome a home it really is,
for now He and I are there, waiting patiently for you.

Good Morning Loving Heart

"Good morning loving heart,"
is what the Lord said to me.
"Today we have so much to do,
Child of Mine, you and Me.

So many that still are lost
and longing to be free.
So many that still don't understand
what they need, is just Me!

So loving heart, I need your smile,
to first just make them feel at ease.
Next I need your voice
to speak MY Word to them, please.

I need your arms to hold them,
and tell them I love them so.
Ok loving heart, are you ready?
Now get up, it's time we have to go!"

A Precious Gift

As I awoke this morning,
I received a precious gift.
It is another day to share
God's love for souls to lift.

See, I really don't deserve it,
this precious gift I am given,
but because of God's love for me,
it is a gift straight from Heaven.

So what is most important,
is to use this gift today,
to share His love with others,
for there truly is no other way.

Life is but a precious gift,
please don't waste what is given.
Remember to share with others today,
praising our Father up in Heaven.

A Difficult Season

A difficult season,
a difficult time.
Nothing seems to go right,
this is what I find.

Problems galore,
come my way.
What can be done
to get me through this day?

So I walked into church
and heard the preacher say,
"Give your life to Christ,
He is the only way!"

So I fell to my knees,
and prayed up above,
"If Jesus You are real,
shower me with Your love."

(continued on next page)

101

So I waited and waited
from Him for a sign.
Then I opened His Word
and this is what I did find.

In the book of John,
Chapter 15, verse nine,
that as the Father loved Him,
Jesus will love us all the time.
(John 15 verse 9 – KJV)

Praise to You, my Lord and Savior,
for my life now belongs to You.
Though difficult seasons will come,
together we will get through them, this is true!

God Is Talking To You Today

God is talking to you today,
He has something important for you to hear,
He wants you to know He loves you,
and that with Him there is nothing to fear.

Listen to Him carefully today,
remove all distractions from your heart,
read from His Holy Scriptures today,
for when you do, you draw nearer, not apart.

God is talking to you today,
He could be doing this by a stranger or a friend.
What He is speaking through them,
is meant just for you, as this day you do begin.

So please listen very carefully,
to each message that He sends your way.
Give Him praise because He loves you so,
that He took His time to talk to you today!

I Want It All

Father, I want it all,
Your Son's life, as well as His death.
Father, I want it all,
the whole, not part of what is left.

I want the resurrection,
as well as the cross.
Father, give me the victory,
as well as the great loss.

Father, I want it all,
for that is what You want to give.
Father, may I have it now,
for in Your Son, Jesus, I want to live.

As in Your Word it is written,
ever since the great fall.
As Jesus said, "I am the Way, the Truth, and the Life",
Father, yes, I want it all!

Broken Hearts Take Time To Mend

A broken heart
takes time to mend,
for if you don't,
it will just break again.

It needs time to grieve
and time to heal,
though the pain will lessen,
it remains so real.

So take this time
to think back and recall,
the happy and fun times
that were shared by all.

Then before you know it
the sadness will end,
because broken hearts
take time to mend.

Now I know what you're thinking,
"How does he know?"
Well, my heart was broke also,
not that long ago!

I Looked For You In Church Today

I looked for you in church today,
but for some reason you were not there.
So the Lord gave me this message,
for with you He wanted me to share.

He knows all about your problems,
and everything you have been going through.
I know He will help you,
for we sang, "God Will Take Care Of You!"

He wants me to tell you,
though in church you were not today,
He will always be with you,
no matter what you do or say.

But what is most important,
that He wanted me to stress to you,
please take some time to spend with Him,
for really any time will do.

Sunday is important,
for that is His day you see,
remember it is all about Him,
not about you and not about me.

So next Sunday I hope to see you,
and together we can worship Him.
May you have a good week,
until Sunday comes again.

When All Was Lost

When all was lost
Jesus was there.
He pulled me from
my pit of despair.

When I thought to myself,
how can I go on?
Jesus said, "Come with Me,
together we will go along."

When love was lost
and my heart cried out,
it was the Son of God
who erased all doubt.

So if you are lost,
and no hope there appears to be,
cry out to Jesus, my friends,
for He was there for me!

He will be there for you, too,
if you only choose Him to be,
don't be a captive to this world,
let Jesus set you free, as He did for me.

It's Never Too Late

Jesus spoke to my heart,
and said, "Tell them for Me,
it's never too late,
if only they will believe!

Please tell them for me,
to tell all others that they may know,
it's never too late,
and that I love them so."

So I said to my Savior,
my blessed Lord above,
"I will do this for You,
because of my love."

So as you read this poem,
the message is so clear,
it's never too late,
if with your heart you will hear.

See, the next breath you take,
could be your last,
your soul would go to hell,
all because you did not ask!

Now pick up your Bible,
and in John 14 verse 6 please read,
Jesus said, "No one comes to the Father,
but by Me!"
(John 14 verse 6 – NKJV)

My friends, it is not too late,
but one day it will.
So come to Jesus now,
He is waiting for you still!

Not About Me But Thee

Another day to give You praise,
for it's not about me, but Thee.
Another time to share Your love,
for that is truly how it must be.

Another chance to help someone,
another person that is in need.
May every action that I do,
prove it's not about me, but Thee.

Another time to share Your Word,
with those that do not know.
Holy Spirit, give me the words to say
just how much I love Thee so.

Another time to say thank You, Lord,
for all you do for me.
How can I not tell all I meet,
"It's not about me, but Thee!

Oh Precious Savior

So many in bondage,
hurting and longing to be free.
Oh precious Savior,
"Why must this be?"

So many looking for something,
a slave to this world of sin.
Oh precious Savior,
"Touch their hearts and enter in!"

So many those are suffering,
disease riddled bodies, minds that are lost!
Oh precious Savior,
"Please, return us to the Cross!"

Oh precious Savior,
please use me today.
Let me tell all in bondage,
"You are the Only Way!"

Oh precious Savior,
I am waiting on You.
"Tell me, touch me, take me,
show me, what can I do?"

Use Me Lord

Here I am, Lord,
ready to do Your will.
Use me, Lord, use me,
quietly, patiently, I am waiting till.

Use my feet to take me
to where Your service will be.
Use my hands, Lord,
reaching out to those in need.

Use my eyes, Lord,
let them search through Your Word.
Use my ears, Lord,
to listen carefully so You can be heard.

Use my mouth, Lord,
that from it Your Spirit can speak.
Use my heart, Lord,
because of You is why it beats.

Use me, Lord, use me,
each day that on this earth I may live.
Use me, Lord, use me,
for my life to You I give.

May You Always Be

May You always be
that light that shines through me.
May You always be
the love that others will see.

May You always be
the first and not the last.
Lord, I thank You, because You have
forgiven me of my past.

May You always be
the goal that I pursue.
May each day that I live
be devoted just to You.

Lord, because of You,
today I am totally free!
My prayer is always Lord,
"May You always be!"

Walk Closely With Jesus Today

Walk closely with Jesus today,
let Him grasp your hand in His.
Look through His eyes of love,
and not your eyes of sin.

Go where He leads you today,
speak healing to those who are sick.
Walk closely with Jesus today,
do not be distracted by the enemies tricks.

Listen to what the Spirit is saying,
not the lies from this world of sin.
Walk closely with Jesus today,
let your heart be one with His.

Be thankful of each step you are taking
because He is showing you the way.
All because of His love for you,
you can walk with Him today!

Jesus Is The Key

How you pray
and what you say
is up to you
each precious day.

The Spirit that lives within,
it is His job to speak to Him.
He takes your words, oh so true,
and pleads to the Father just for you.

The Father sees just the heart
and knows your needs before you start.
He waits for what the Spirit pleads,
then grants your wishes, this you must believe.

But the most important part so true,
is to ask in Jesus name for you.
To have your prayer answered this must be,
See my friends, "Jesus is the key!"

May It Not Be Too Late

May it not be too late
that you will truly believe.
May you understand as I do,
it's through Christ, the Spirit you'll receive.

May you wait no longer
and on your knees may you find,
the true love of Jesus
and leave your old life behind.

May it not be too late
for the next minute it might,
take nothing for granted,
we must walk by faith, not by sight!

May it not be too late
is also my prayer.
If they look in your heart,
will they find Jesus there?

Don't wait till the end
to make up your mind.
I'll ask once again,
in your heart, will Jesus they find?

Has God Got Your Attention

Has God got your attention yet?
He is waiting on you!
He created you for a reason,
He has work for you to do.

Has God got your attention yet?
If not, what more does He has to do?
What will it take for you to realize,
it is about Him, not about you!

See, He loves you so much
that He gives and gives and gives.
In return all He wants from us
is our obedience to Him as we live.

My friends, He got my attention,
so many, many years ago.
My life is for Him now,
because I love Him so.

So please don't wait any longer,
always remember this important question,
when things are happening in your life,
"Is God trying to get my attention?"

Get Your Eyes Off Yourself

"Get your eyes off yourself
and put them on Me",
is what the Lord's message is,
for so all can see.

He is our provider,
giving us all that we will need,
"Ask and it will be given to you",
is His Word to you and me.

Don't worry about tomorrow,
but who you can help today.
That is how life was meant to live,
as you go about your way.

So I know what you are thinking,
"Who will watch out for me?"
Well, that is for Jesus and someone else,
yes, that is the way it was meant to be.

Rejoice And Learn

For every trial
that comes your way,
rejoice and learn
from it today.

Whether it be
good or bad,
give thanks and understand
and be glad you have.

Watch what others
are going through.
Reach out to help
those in trouble too.

Rejoice and learn
in what you do,
yes, thank Him for
your troubles too.

We learn as we live
life day by day.
We rejoice because He loves us,
teach me Lord, is what I pray!

I Will Follow You

Wherever You want me to go,
whatever You want me to do,
Lord, hear my cry,
I will follow You!

Whatever the task You have for me,
wherever it may be,
Lord, I am your willing servant,
waiting to follow Thee.

Whenever You will call me,
just tell me what to do.
Lord, use me to do Your bidding,
before my life is through.

My life is all Yours now,
my love for You is true.
Wherever You are going,
please Lord, let me go with You!

Do You Know Me

There came a cry from Heaven,
it was real for all to see.
The Creator of Everything said,
"Do you really know Me?

Moment by moment,
day by day,
I give you everything
and yet you turn away.

I always watch over you,
wherever you may go.
I will answer your every prayer
because I love you so.

All I want is your love in return
for that is how it must be.
I will always be here waiting,
Do you really know Me?"

Get Down On Your Knees

Get down on your knees,
if you truly believe,
cry out to our Lord above!

He is waiting to hear
that we need Him here,
we can't live without His love.

Get down on your knees,
and let Him know,
this is how we truly feel.

He is waiting for each
to cry from the heart
and say, "Lord, this is how we feel!"

Get down on your knees
and stay there awhile,
listen quietly for His voice.

He is waiting on you
to love Him too,
see, He made the first choice!

Be Blessed Today

Be blessed today,
for He is always with you.
When the day seems long,
He will get you through.

Be blessed today,
for you are truly His.
Because of His love,
His blessings He gives.

Be blessed today
and give praise above.
What will it cost you?
Nothing but your love!

Be blessed today,
He really wants you to be.
See, He is waiting to bless you,
but first you must believe.

Believe in Him,
and what His Word does say,
for that is when you will
be blessed today!

While The Preacher Was Preaching

While the preacher was preaching
in church today,
the Lord spoke to my heart,
and this is what He had to say.

"Talk to Me, my child,
tell Me, what is it that you wish?"
I replied, "Lord, do You have the time,
for I have quite a list?"

I felt His smile
come upon His face,
then He did say, "Of course,
you came to the right place!"

So I started to pour
my heart out to Him,
then I thought of so many,
that are still living in sin.

I paused for a moment
and then I did say,
"Forgive me Lord,
it's not about me, but for Your lost I pray!

You know my heart
and I know Yours,
but so many still don't know You
after all these years.

So I know You will bless me
and not many will I miss,
please move your lost,
to the top of my list."

Then within the moment,
I felt God's love to so many reaching.
See, God granted my wish,
while the preacher was preaching!

Which Way Are You Going

Another day is upon us,
another decision to be made.
My question to you is,
"Which way are you going today?"

God will always be there,
for that will never change.
See, He will not force you
to choose Himself, as your way.

He is a daily choice,
that each one must make,
you cannot go with Him
and stay in the same place.

Which way are you going?
The choice is up to you.
He has work that is waiting,
something that only you can do.

So, which way are you going?
I pray it is with God and me.
There is a lot to say and do,
choose, then come and see!

Why Do I Do It

I am a servant of the Lord,
that is truly what I want to be.
Everything I do is for Him
and nothing is done for me.

Everything I need or will ever want,
He supplies all for me.
So why should I worry about this,
He takes care of everything, you see.

All I do is what He wants,
touching others just like Him,
once you get your eyes off yourself,
well, that's when life truly begins.

So if you wonder, "Why do I do it?"
I hope you can tell by my grin,
I do because He loves me,
I do it because I love Him!

When It Is All Said And Done

When it is all said and done
and my life on earth is through,
my greatest achievement on this earth
is Lord, that I spoke of You.

When it is all said and done
and no more that my eyes will see,
my greatest joy will be
that You walked with me.

When it is all said and done
and at Your throne I bow in love,
my greatest wish would be,
to see friends and family gathered with me above.

But that is a decision that must be made,
separately by each and everyone.
We will not know for sure until
when it is all said and done.

One Day

One day it will be,
just as Your Word promised me,
the greatest day to behold,
walking streets paved in gold.

One day will finally come
when pain and sorrow will be no more,
for on that glorious day
I will enter Heaven's door.

One day not far ahead,
known only to the Father above,
I will finally be home,
all because of His Son's love.

So until that day arrives,
I have much work to do,
to tell all about Him,
so they can be there too!

Be Blessed This Day

Be blessed this day
as you go on your way.
Understand that it is from Him!

Be blessed this day
in a special way,
because He loves to give.

Be blessed this day
as with thanks you say,
"I am not deserving of."

Be blessed this day
as on your knees you pray
to our wonderful Father above.

Be blessed this day
listen to what I say,
"First you must believe.

Whatever blessing comes your way,
be blessed this day,
because of Jesus, you did receive!"

Birthdays

Every time we celebrate a birthday,
oh Lord, I pray that we all will see.
It was because and from You,
that is what each birthday must be.

Oh, it is a time to celebrate,
but to You we must give our praise.
For You gave us another year
to tell someone about You, each and every day.

All the presents are great
that we will receive.
But the best one is Your love,
given freely for all who will believe.

So thank You for this birthday, Lord,
that we celebrate once a year.
May all the days between them
be blessings from You, for with others to share.

The Shepherd

The Shepherd went out to the field
to look for His sheep.
He noticed one was missing
and started to weep.

Why was one so important?
Was it more special than all the rest?
No, He loved each and everyone
and to each He gives them His best.

So out into the pasture,
the Shepherd did go.
He looked and looked
because He loved the lost so.

See, the moral of this poem is
it did not matter what had to be done,
for until the lost one was found,
he is the special one.

So if you are lost,
cry out and do not stop.
See, the Shepherd is looking
to bring you back to the flock.

Not When But Where

Ashes to ashes
and dust to dust,
since they had to go,
then I guess I must!

Oh, we will go
and that's for sure.
The question is not when
but where I hear.

Some like it hot and
for some it will be.
I prefer the other, that
the good Lord promised me.

Now if I am wrong,
then I have nothing to lose.
But if I am right, the non-believers will,
because they didn't choose.

So read this poem carefully
and from the Bible also read,
John 14 verse 6 where Jesus says,
"No one comes to the Father but by Me."

(John 14 verse 6 – NKJV)

He Is With You

He is with you,
if you want Him or not.
He is waiting for You
by each tick of the clock.

Each second you breathe,
He is there very true.
Why you may ask?
Simply because of His love for you.

He died on the cross,
as He hung there in shame,
and guess what my friends,
we were all to blame.

"Forgive them, Father",
was what He said,
"This is Jesus, King of the Jews",
was nailed above His head.

And still He is with You,
no matter what you do,
see, He will not leave, for He's
waiting for you to choose.

We Shall Not Be Always

We shall not be always
struggling and living in sin.
We shall not be always
because of Christ's love within.

We shall not be always
fighting sickness all around.
We shall not be always
because in Christ healing is found.

We shall not be always
living in a world without love.
We shall not be always
because of our Father's promise above.

We shall not be always
not knowing what the end might be.
We shall not be always
for in God's Word it's written, you see.

We shall not be always
for this is so true.
We shall not be always,
I believe, what about you?

What Can I Do

"What can I do?"
"What can I do?"
Is a question asked
of the Lord, by many of you.

"Where do I start
to do Your will?"
Is another question asked,
but you remain still.

"Who should I talk with,
where do I go?
Please tell me, Lord,
so that I may know."

Then as you ask these questions,
you pass homeless people in the street.
As you look at the ground,
you see no shoes on their feet.

In the grocery store,
where you always go,
you hear a mother tell her kids,
"We can't afford it, so the answer is no!"

You raise your head above
and say, "Lord, what can I do?"
The Lord answers you lovingly,
"Would it make a difference if I told you?"

Life Is A Collection Of Memories

Life is a collection of memories,
that we get from the choices we've made.
For some there are more bad then good,
and it hurts when we think back how we behaved.

But for some there are a lot of good ones,
each one better than the last.
Thank God for those memories, my friends,
for this life goes by so very fast.

Don't be discouraged if the good ones,
when you think back are only a few.
Just be thankful to the Lord above,
each new day may bring a good memory for you.

So the moral of this poem
Is, don't wait until the end.
Start making the right choices now,
what you collect, is up to you, my friend!

Our Great Physician

Our heavenly Father
is our great Physician,
He guides the doctors
through His divine wisdom.

Each earthly body
without windows He did make,
for by the stripes on Jesus back,
all illness He did break.

So when in your body,
you do feel sick,
get on your knees,
and begin to pray quick.

Grab onto your Bible
and from His Word please read,
Isaiah 53:5 "and with His stripes we are healed."
My friends, all we have to do is believe!

(Isaiah 53:5 – KJV)

One Nail That I Hold

One nail that I hold in my hand,
it is one nail of three.
One nail to remind me always,
of how my Savior died for me.

One nail that I hold in my hand,
it really does matter to me.
It is one nail of three,
that held Him to that tree.

One nail that I hold in my hand,
the importance I wish many would see,
with Easter quickly approaching,
it represents His love for you and me.

The moral of this poem,
there is Salvation in it to behold,
it bonds Jesus to me through love,
with this one nail that I hold!

The Day Was Coming

The day was coming,
the cross was getting near,
but it had to be done,
to erase everyone's fear.

The night was black,
cold was in the air,
but the love of Jesus
conquered all that was there.

What is pain to us is nothing,
compared to what was put upon Him.
And why He did it,
was to put an end to sin.

But what hurt the most,
as it probably still does today,
was on the Cross,
like us, His Father looked away.

So as Easter draws near,
make each day mean for something,
Think of how Jesus must have felt,
for He knew the day was coming.

A Message From The Great Physician

The Lord said to me,
"Please listen and don't ask why.
If you want to be healthy
watch what you put inside.

If you don't want to cook
for there's no time to prepare,
then the consequences are,
have your body be aware.

See, your weight will increase
from all the fat.
Your heart will slow down,
and your brain will forget where it's at.

Your body will creek,
and you will have pains in your bones.
Your digestive system will scream,
please just leave me alone.

(continued on next page)

Sickness will come
and much longer it will last.
The immune system I gave you
will be just a thing of the past.

All the medical people
you will know by their first name.
Instead of good food, it is pills you eat.
Now tell Me the truth, isn't that a shame?

So put down all those chips
and throw out all those cakes.
Start eating more veggies and salads,
come on, give your body a break.

So if you do not listen
to what I am telling you,
you might get to meet Me sooner,
than I intended for you."

Face The Facts

Face the facts
because they are true.
Pick up the Bible and read
what God is telling you.

Face the facts,
when troubles you see.
For Jesus said, "Trials and tribulations
there will surely be."

Face the facts,
of what this life must be,
Jesus said, "Pick up your cross,
and follow Me!"

Face the facts
where it is written,
it is only through Jesus,
that we can enter Heaven.

Face the facts
and just believe,
God's gift of love,
through grace you freely receive.

God's Word was written,
so through the ages it would last.
Now it's up to you, believe,
and face the facts!

My Book Of Life

As I came to the gates of Heaven,
St. Peter said,
"You have to answer a question
before I let you in!"
I wondered of all the questions
He would ask,
what would it be,
before my life there would begin?

Then St. Peter opened a large book,
on each page was what I did
on earth with pictures to see.
Then He asked me this question,
"If you had to do it all over,
what would it be?"

As I looked at all the pictures
that represented my earthly life,
I saw my childhood, my mom and dad
and my brothers, I saw my kids,
my grandkids and my wife.

I saw all the smiles,
all the laughter, and the fun,
but I also saw all the heartache,
all the crying, and the tears.
I saw all the hurting either I did,
or someone did to me,
year after year after year.

I saw myself being very busy,
trying to create a very good life.
But then I also saw
all the times I was away,
that I didn't spend
with my kids and my wife.

Then I saw all the friends
I have known,
that through the years
I did lose touch.
Though I didn't have many friends
as some might,
the ones I had, I cared for very much.

But then my eyes got brighter,
what I saw was my walk with God.
I knew at that very moment
the answer to the question,
I wouldn't change anything,
for I might lose that, if I had.

See, this life is about learning
and as we do, the choices that we make,
but the most important is choosing Him,
for it is a life with Him in Heaven,
that is at stake.

So if this poem does nothing else,
than to make you stop and take a look,
I pray in the pictures of your life
you see God,
just like I saw in my book!

I Came Upon

I came upon a hungry man,
looking for something to eat.
He said, "I don't have anything,
I am hungry as can be!"

Jesus said, "Do you see him?"
I said, "Yes, Lord, I do see!"
Jesus said, When you look upon him
you are really seeing Me!"

I came upon an addict,
drugs consuming his every move.
He said, "This is all I have now,
what can I do?"

Jesus said, "Do you see him?"
I said, "Yes, Lord, I do see!"
Jesus said, "When you look upon him
you are really seeing Me!"

I came upon a homeless man,
his home was now the street.
He said, "Everything I once had,
I've lost, woe is me!"

Jesus said, "Do you see him?"
I said, "Yes, Lord, I do see!"
Jesus said, When you look upon him,
you are really seeing Me!"

I came upon a mirror,
then in the reflection I did see,
a hungry, homeless, addicted, person,
what I saw in the mirror was me.

So the moral of this poem,
is that we are each one in the same.
We are all created in God's image
and Jesus is our name.

This sinful world is our exterior,
what we let it do to us we will be.
But Jesus can change all that,
if you will only just believe, He did for me!

Get Up And Rest

"Get up and rest,"
is what God says,
"get up and wait on Me.

Be prepared
for the work ahead
with rested eyes you may see.

Get up and rest,
do not start out
a journey on your own.

Be quiet and still,
waiting till you hear
directions from My Throne.

Get up and rest,
for strength you'll need
to fight what comes your way.

The enemy is strong,
the battle is long
and is for sure to come today.

Get up and rest
and be assured,
in Me a victor you will be."

Wait on Me,
oh child of Mine,
get up, rest and see.

The Wish

I opened up an email today,
it said to make a wish.
Then it said it would come true,
if I sent it on to all on my list.

Then within the moment,
God said, "What would be even more smart,
for it is not about how many or who you send to,
but what you ask in prayer, from your heart.

Also what is most important
for your wish to come true,
is to ask in My Son's name,
then what you ask for, will be given to you."

Now here I believe is the catch
that many a person will miss.
If it's not to bring glory to God,
why even make a wish?

Lost Angels

This is a poem for all the Lost Angels,
created by God above.
So many had to leave so soon,
but left such an imprint of love.

Why their stay was so short,
or why we had to suffer such pain,
thank You Heavenly Father,
just that the Lost Angels came.

Just to have a life touched
by Your love from above,
if just for a minute or a lifetime,
a love is always a love.

So one day Lost Angels,
I am not sure when that will be,
we will all be together again,
this time for all of eternity!

In The Blink Of An Eye

In the blink of an eye,
death passed by,
with my new eyes I began to see.

My old life was gone,
now with Jesus I belong,
living together in all eternity.

In the blink of an eye,
every year passed by,
no more living with worry and sin.

Just as in the Bible it said,
don't worry what lies ahead,
just have faith in Him.

In the blink of an eye,
all was changed,
no more tears or hurting there would be.

What most think is the end
is just the start, my friend,
if in Jesus you do believe.

Jesus, Jesus, Precious Jesus

Jesus, Jesus, precious Jesus,
please be with me today.
Though I do not deserve Your love,
it is mine through grace to claim.

Jesus, Jesus, precious Jesus,
may my heart to You be pure.
It is a choice that I must make,
so that in this life You will insure.

Jesus, Jesus, precious Jesus,
please use me to do Thy will.
My life has no meaning, it is true,
except with You until.

Jesus, Jesus, precious Jesus,
without You what would I do?
Jesus, Jesus, precious Jesus,
my Lord and Savior, I love You!

Life Is A Choice

I woke up this morning,
not knowing what to do.
My friends, life is a choice,
it is all up to you.

You can walk in the Son-light,
or be lost in the dark.
My friends, life is a choice,
it is a matter of the heart.

Each day can be a struggle,
or you can be a blessing indeed.
My friends, life is a choice,
it is what you choose to believe.

Oh there will be troubles,
but remember all is not lost.
My friends, life is a choice,
for me I chose Jesus and His Cross!

Why Did They Do It

Why did they do it?
Why did they die for me?
Why did they give up their precious life
just so I could be free?

Why did they do it?
The ultimate sacrifice that was made.
They didn't even know me,
yet all they had they gave!

Why did they do it?
Because others did it for them.
It is called "giving",
no matter what be the outcome or the end.

Sacrifice is a gift,
no matter what the cost.
To fully understand it's meaning,
we must just look to the Cross!

Cries From Within

Many, many people
living in this world of sin,
looking up to the heavens with
cries from within.

Their hearts are uneasy,
unhappy where they've been,
looking up to the heavens with
cries from within.

They are looking for the Answer
for in this life they want to win,
looking up to the heavens with
cries from within.

Their hearts cry out for God's love,
they need the Spirit to enter in.
Oh why doesn't God hear these
cries from within?

Well, I believe God hears all cries,
but we must first surrender all to Him.
See, once I laid all at His feet, He answered my
cries from within!

Share

If He has given you a smile to wear,
then it was given to you to share.

If He has blessed you today in some way,
it is because through Jesus, the blessing was paid.

If He has lessened your burden to be,
it is because to help others, who need to be free.

If He has filled your heart with love,
it is to share with others, His love from above.

If He has given you strength to complete each task,
it is so you may share your strength,
when others do ask.

See, whatever He gives you,
because He loves you and cares,
it was given to you, so with others you will gladly share.

It was not given to you for you alone to keep,
it was given to share, then His blessings you will reap!

Time Is Short

Time is short,
opportunities are passing by,
so many still must understand,
each must choose to receive life's wonderful prize.

A gift that is given
must be first received.
It must first be accepted
and then through love, believed!

See, time is short,
for so many that still don't know,
it's not about this life,
but Jesus, who loves us so!

So whatever time is left,
and only the Father knows that day,
if you believe as it is written,
spread the gospel message and don't forget to pray!

You Can Make A Difference

You can make a difference
even when the enemy tells you "no".
You can make a difference
because Jesus loves you so!

You can make a difference
yes, with Jesus, you can make things right.
You can make a difference
for you are so precious in His sight.

You can make a difference,
see the choice is up to you.
You can make a difference
in everything that you do.

So decide today, my friends,
surrendering your life to Him is the key.
You can make a difference,
you may be the only Jesus that someone ever sees!

Look Up

I once was hurt,
I had no place to turn.
I had a pain in my heart
that would constantly burn.

I fell to the ground,
I could not get up,
then my gracious Lord and Savior said,
"My Child, please look up!"

See, I was face down,
I had no other place to go.
I was empty and helpless,
I thought I was in this world alone.

So if this ever happens
and you feel this way too,
remember to look up,
for Jesus is waiting for you.

The Powers In You

Please listen, my friends,
before this day is through,
whatever you are up against
the Powers in you.

Once you accept Christ
to come into your heart
and surrender your life to Him,
then His power imparts.

Whatever comes against you,
and in this world plenty there will be,
you have the power to beat it,
the Powers in you, it's Jesus you see.

So don't give up hope,
and your victory please claim,
the powers in you,
claim it, in Jesus name!!!

In Jesus Name

Another day
my eyes opened to see,
there is work to be done
for my Lord through me.

There are people to see
and places to go,
another day
to tell all He loves them so.

Another day
to tell this world,
it is all about Him
as written in His Word.

Yes another day
He has given to me,
to witness for Him
so all can see.

They have nothing to loose
and Heaven to gain.
Praise God, yes, another day,
I claim it, in Jesus name!!!

You Came To Me

I said to the Lord, "My heart is broken,
the hurt is so strong,
please help me now
for I can't go on!

Whatever You do,
please do it fast.
Make the hurt stop,
please don't let it last."

Then as I was quiet
He said, "Listen to Me.
The last time your heart was broke
didn't I set you free?

See pains will come,
heartbreaks there will be.
What is most important is,
you came to Me!"

Sooner Than Later

Sooner or later
our bodies will fail.
The light will get dimmer,
our skin will grow pale.

Sooner or later
our legs will give out.
Our breath will grow shallow,
we won't even be able to shout.

Sooner or later,
which one will it be?
Well, it really doesn't matter,
for it's not up to us you see.

Oh, we will try to eat healthy
and exercise when we can,
but it's not about the sooner or the later,
it is all about God's plan.

See, being Christians and believers,
there is nothing that could be greater.
I pray all will find out,
yes, sooner than later!

Life Changes

One day you're happy,
then one day you're sad.
One day you can lose
all that you have.

One day all seems so clear,
then one day you're in a fog.
You say to yourself,
"How can all go so wrong?"

Life changes my friends,
by what sometimes we choose.
Maybe what you decide today,
could be why tomorrow you may lose.

But praise be to God
when life changes come our way,
for He never changes,
day after day after day.

A Minute To Win It

A minute to win it
or a lifetime instead.
Be careful for we don't know
when this life will really end.

A minute to win it
or a life with Christ you can lose.
It really all comes down to
what is it that you choose.

See, everyone can be a winner
and sadly many are not.
For to win is Jesus,
He is what winning and life is all about.

So take a minute now,
think of it, as it was your last.
Did you win or did you lose?
That minute is now in the past!

The Animals Really Knew

The star was over Bethlehem
and the manger was all aglow.
Mary, Joseph and the Christ Child,
side by side in the hay, all in a row.

Then came the three Wise men,
kneeling with their gifts from afar.
They came to see this Special One,
by following Bethlehem's star.

Not many in the city
knew why this Child had come.
But it appeared that the animals knew,
as they looked at each other, one by one.

Yes, they knew Him as their Creator,
and the One who gives them food.
He also gave them shelter,
oh yes, the animals really knew.

See, the animals knew more that the humans
because they just rely on need.
Maybe one day we could be as smart,
all it takes is to truly believe!

Blessed Memories

I looked for your cardinals,
but they were nowhere to be found.
I watched the snow fall from the sky
and then gently kiss the ground.

I walked the paths that we did walk,
together, hand in hand,
but some of the beauty I no longer see
in this, God's winter wonderland.

For your beauty is no longer here with me,
it is just God's beauty now to behold.
He blessed me with your memory
on that day He called you home.

But we will always be together,
for in love there is no other way.
One day I will be called home too,
thank You Jesus, for that day!

What I Have, He Gave

What I have, He gave.
I got nothing on my own.
The air I breathe and water I drink
come from Him and Him alone.

The food I eat, the clothes I wear,
all from my Savior above.
The family and friends that are in my life,
He gave so I could understand and experience love.

The money I earn so that I can live
is what He provided to me.
All He asked is to give 10% back,
so through His church more would see.

They will see it is all His,
because of His love, He gave.
And the most important gift we get,
each one of our souls, if we ask, He saves!

On The Way To The Cross

On the way to the Cross
He thought about us,
He loved us through
His hurting and His pain.

But it had to be done
for the victory to be won,
so that through His death
we all will gain.

Though not many would know
and their actions did show,
that for so many
it was just all for naught.

But His Word was left
so that all could get,
loves lesson and truth
could be taught.

On the way to the Cross
Jesus thought of us,
He said, "Father,
please just blame Me!"

(continued on next page)

Let Me take Your wrath
so this can be their path,
to be with us
through all Eternity.

So His Father agreed
and said, "Son come to Me,
You have done My will
so they all can be free.

They now have the task
all they must do is ask
Jesus, my Lord
and Savior, please be!"

Yes, through the Cross
Jesus proved His love for us,
all we have to do
is just believe!

Going Back

Every breath we take is from the present
thanks to God it does not lack.
But every now and then there are times
I wished I could go back!

Back to friends and family
and times that made me smile.
Back to places I liked to visit
oh yes, just for a little while.

Back to times when I felt at peace
and also not so old.
Back to see love ones that are gone,
the ones we no longer can hold.

But we know this wish can never be
and God also knew from the start.
So in each child of His,
He gave them a special heart.

A heart that will always hold memories
with space that will never lack.
All because of His love for us,
He gave us a way to go back!

Nothing Has Really Changed

Over 2000 years have gone by
and God's reason is still the same.
He came to this earth as man,
and to show, that "His love" will never change.

His love is for the wealthy and famous,
just as it is for the unknown and the poor.
It is for the strong and healthy,
also the weak, the sick and many more.

See, His love isn't tied to a situation
or what in life your status may be.
No, it is all about "Him" my friends,
not you, and not me.

See, nothing has really changed,
since God created us with His love.
It's not about, who, where or what you are
but because He loves us so much.

Yep, that much that He suffered,
though it didn't have to be,
people were yelling "Crucify him",
people like you and like me.

Well, His love hasn't changed,
now it's "2019", and it never will.
It doesn't matter how many years go by,
He loved us in the beginning and loves us still!

Easter Sunday

Forget the Easter Bunny,
remember the stone that was rolled away.
Forget the colored Easter eggs,
remember we celebrate "our risen Savior" today!

Remember the price Jesus paid,
for your sins and mine.
Forget all the worldly influences
and satan's constant lies.

Remember if Jesus was not resurrected
then His death was all in vain.
He was the innocent Lamb of God,
His resurrection is why He came.

When He said, "Father please forgive them",
He meant every word.
when He said, "It is finished",
those were the sweetest words ever heard.

So this is Easter Sunday,
we are blessed to celebrate once again.
Forget what happened in the past,
remember Easter Sunday is where it all began.

If you are not sure
and still are in doubt,
Pick up God's Holy Word,
its all there my friends, check it out!

The Bible

The Bible can not help you
if you leave it on the shelf.
It was meant as a means of living
and also when you need help.

It is God's true Word
that the Holy Spirit inspired others to write.
As we read and live what it says
we are so precious in His sight.

But one thing to keep in mind
as each scripture you do read,
without the Holy Spirit in you,
it appears to be foolishness indeed.

So the choice is up to each of us
it will change our lives if we believe it.
First ask Jesus in your heart,
then pick up His Word and "read it"!

The Answers

My friends today we live
in a "me", "me", "me" time.
When in reality it always has been
"His", "His", "His" time to shine.

We have stopped looking for others
that are hurting and in need.
Everywhere we look it screams,
what about "me", "me", "me'!

Family life is crumbling
even before our own eyes.
Lives are being consumed by
deceitfulness and lies.

Addiction and sickness appears
to be all around.
Love and kindness is very
seldom to be found.

But fear not my friends
for everything is not all lost.
Redemption will always be found
nailed to the cross.

We each have the power within us
to change our selfish lives around.
Pick up God's Word my friends
there the answers will be found.

True Love

It seemed like it ended so quickly
almost before it began
then I realized it was only
just a one sided plan.

One side where love flowed
and with no ending in sight.
But the love that flowed so freely
came from only one which wasn't right.

For a love to truly grow and blossom
it must be like a circle appear
for what one gives out
must come back and thats for sure.

So when you truly find love
and comes flowing back to you
work on keeping it stronger
for with true love that's what you must do.

Life's Remote

Life has no remote
on Facebook I did read
you have to change it yourself
is what it also said to me.

Then within a few minutes
the Lord spoke to my heart
He said everything that you need
is with you from the start.

What is important to understand
as we go through what is called life,
each one of us must choose
either what is wrong or what is right.

We each were given eyes
so from His Word we can read
and ears to listen before we choose
what we want our lives to be.

If you choose what's wrong
after seeing or hearing the Truth,
then there is consequences
that you will then go through.

Oh yes, one thing to keep in mind
your lives battery will eventually wear out.
It will be too late then to want to change,
sorry my friends, but that is what life is about.

It's Not Too Late

I thought about all the chances
that I never did see.
Opportunities that I missed
to say what you mean to me.

Things that I could of done
to show along our way,
what you meant in my life
but I never took the time each day.

So this is another Thanksgiving,
to be thankful as can be.
It should also be just another day
to not miss what is important to see.

Family, friends and blessings from above,
that is what makes our lives so great.
My Thanksgiving prayer for all,
I pray it's not too late.

Another Day Somewhere

As I looked out my window
my neighbors house I could not see.
It was snowing so hard
that it was blinding me.

Now if I was in the South
for sure not much snow as here,
but with a hurricane
would the neighbors house even be there?

I guess wherever you live
there are adjustments you must make
for there could be flooding, fires, hurricanes,
or blizzards, that sure don't make life great.

So grab a shovel, a hose, a sandbag
or onto something hold tight.
It might be one of these,
that gets you through the night.

So I believe what it all comes down to
no matter where you choose to live
be grateful to our God above
another day somewhere, to you, He did give!

There They Knelled

I watched a televised football game
many children's heroes knelled.
The song played was the National Anthem
and to many it all looked so unreal.

Why are they doing this
must be running through their minds.
Whatever happened to respecting the flag
that many died for and some even were left behind.

I wonder what our Founding Fathers would say
if they could look at this and see.
So many disrespecting what others died for
listen my friends, not a sports game but to be free.

What God must be thinking
for when looking down from above.
See, He blessed this country of ours
and proved it with His love.

Well, one thing I can imagine
and I am sure God would probably say,
while your down there "boys", yep, not men,
it would be smart to think of Me and pray!!!!

We Don't Have All The Answers

We don't have all the answers
and I guess that is God's way.
Sometimes we think we know so much
and then it all goes astray.

There are times in our life
that we just can't understand.
Something or someone is taken from us,
is it by God's loving hand?

The hurting never seems to leave
but seems to lessen in some days.
But still the question lingers on
could there of been another way?

Was there something more I could of done?
Wasn't my love enough?
I raise my eyes toward Heaven
and say, "Lord, I need Your special touch!"

The answer is just for You to know
the question is all mine.
One day as it is written,
"You will make all things known, yes, in time."

Outside The Walls

It is hard to witness to someone
one hour on Sunday morning.
It is very unlikely the Holy Spirit
will bring many there without warning.

Church is good to come once a week
to learn, sing, worship and give praise.
But you have to look outside the walls
for those that the Lord sends your way.

Look for those hurting, poor, confused,
yes, anyone in need of His loving touch.
Look for those that have less than you,
knowing that you care can mean so much.

See, if you truly have Jesus in your heart
it is Him what others need and will see.
If you yield yourself to the Holy Spirit
through you He can really set the captives free.

So to all you one hour on Sunday, Christians,
it is outside the walls you must be.
Don't wait for another Sunday to come
then think, is this is all God wants from me?

What Will I See

What will I see after I am gone?
Will the life I lived be a blessing to someone?
Will there be tears because I am no longer there?
Did a life or many I pray changed, because I cared?

What will I see to show I was there?
Will there be kind words spoken or heard anywhere?
Will a smile appear on each one's face,
when my name is mentioned from place to place?

What will I see I am curious to know?
Please tell me my love touched a life or maybe even you?
It is important to understand and for me to see
was my life used to the best it could be?

God has a reason why each one is here.
It is up to each to discover and then to share.
He gave us all gifts that He wrapped with His Grace
for once we choose will sure put a smile on His face.

So I know what is important and what I will see
it will be God's smiling face looking at me.
His arms will be wide open as far as can be
from His lips He will say well done, that's what I'll see!

Being Like Christ

It goes against my grain to lie.
It goes against my grain to curse.
It goes against my grain to displease Him,
of all these this hurts me the worse.

I am encouraged to read the Word.
I am encouraged to speak for Him.
I am encouraged to share the Gospel message,
from the beginning to the end.

I listen to the Spirit
and let Him guide my way.
I have a wonderful relationship,
what more can I say.

So if you want to be like Christ
for me this is what it is.
See it is not about our lives
it is for sure all about His!

God's Loving Hands

The sunshine lifts me up.
The rain softens my fall.
The storms in my life,
makes me seek You more.

The light covers darkness.
The warmth hides the cold.
Love conquered emptiness
changing this heart of stone.

Smiles covered frowns.
Laughter ceased the tears.
Singing lets my soul speak
as I live out the years.

So as you read this poem
I pray you understand,
everything listed in it
comes from God's loving hands.

What Is Love

I raised my eyes above and asked God,
"What is love, what can it be?"
Jesus said, "Get your eyes off yourself,
look around, look for Me!"

He said, "Look for those that are hurting
and they have nowhere to turn.
Look to those that are hungry
and for food their bodies does yearn.

Look for those whose addictions
on their lives have taken hold.
Look for those who live on the streets
for they have nowhere to go.

Look for those consumed with anger,
for somewhere in their lives they been betrayed.
Look for those that life has little meaning,
as they live out their lives day by day."

All at once the answer became clear
as I prayed and gave thanks to our Father above.
Love is letting His Spirit flow through me,
reaching out to those still questioning, "what is love?"

Then He said, "Keep searching each day,
for the hurting and the lost,
this is the reason for the Christmas season,
and also why I went to the Cross!"

Use this page to list your favorite poems
with their page number!

MArsha
Blackburn
Tenn.